Crypto Investing

A Comprehensive Guide for Beginners

By: Daviid Mouscho

Contents

Introduction:
Why Crypto Investing Matters

Crypto investing matters for several reasons, and its significance can vary depending on individual perspectives and goals. Here are some key reasons why crypto investing matters:

Financial Inclusion: Cryptocurrency provides access to financial services for individuals who are unbanked or underbanked. This is particularly important in regions where traditional banking infrastructure is lacking or unreliable.

Decentralization: Cryptocurrencies are typically not controlled by a central authority or government. This decentralization can provide a sense of autonomy and security, especially in environments with political instability or economic crises.

Innovation: The underlying technology of cryptocurrencies, blockchain, has the potential to revolutionize various industries beyond finance, such as supply chain management, healthcare, and voting systems. By investing in cryptocurrencies, individuals support the development and adoption of this innovative technology.

Diversification: Cryptocurrencies offer an alternative asset class for investment portfolios. Diversifying into cryptocurrencies can help spread risk and potentially enhance overall portfolio performance, especially during times of economic uncertainty.

Hedge Against Inflation: Some investors turn to cryptocurrencies like Bitcoin as a hedge against traditional fiat currency devaluation and inflation. The limited supply of cryptocurrencies can make them resistant to inflationary pressures.

Global Accessibility: Cryptocurrencies can be bought, sold, and transferred across borders with relative ease. This global accessibility can be valuable for international trade, remittances, and cross border transactions.

Speculative Potential: Cryptocurrencies have demonstrated the potential for significant price appreciation in a relatively short period. This potential for high returns attracts speculators and investors seeking opportunities for profit.

Financial Education: Engaging in crypto investing can be an educational experience, helping individuals learn about economics, financial markets, and emerging technologies.

Community Empowerment: Cryptocurrency communities often emphasize principles of decentralization, self-sovereignty, and peer to peer collaboration. Participating in these communities can foster a sense of empowerment and social responsibility.

Evolution of Money: Cryptocurrencies challenge traditional notions of money and how value is exchanged. They represent a potential shift in the way societies transact and store value, making it an area of interest for those exploring the future of finance.

It's essential to note that crypto investing also comes with risks and challenges, including market volatility, regulatory uncertainty, and security concerns. Therefore, individuals considering crypto investments should conduct thorough research, understand the risks, and make informed decisions based on their financial goals and risk tolerance.

In summary, crypto investing matters because it offers opportunities for financial inclusion, innovation, diversification, and financial empowerment, while also challenging traditional financial systems and providing potential solutions to various global economic challenges. However, it is not without risks, and individuals should approach it with caution and due diligence.

The Potential and The Risks

Crypto investing presents both significant potential and notable risks, making it a dynamic and complex asset class. Understanding these aspects is crucial for anyone considering investing in cryptocurrencies.

Potential of Crypto Investing:

High Returns: Cryptocurrencies have demonstrated the potential for substantial returns on investment. Early investors in cryptocurrencies like Bitcoin and Ethereum have seen significant price appreciation.

Diversification: Adding cryptocurrencies to an investment portfolio can provide diversification benefits, potentially reducing overall portfolio risk. Cryptocurrencies often have low correlations with traditional assets like stocks and bonds.

Decentralization and Security: Blockchain technology, the foundation of cryptocurrencies, offers secure and transparent transaction methods. The decentralized nature of blockchain can reduce the risk of fraud and censorship.

Financial Inclusion: Cryptocurrencies can provide access to financial services for individuals who are unbanked or underbanked, especially in regions with limited banking infrastructure.

Innovation: Beyond digital currencies, blockchain technology has the potential to revolutionize various industries, such as supply chain management, healthcare, and voting systems. Investing in cryptocurrencies can support the development of these innovations.

Risks of Crypto Investing:

Volatility: Cryptocurrencies are known for their extreme price volatility. Prices can fluctuate significantly over short periods, leading to substantial gains or losses.

Regulatory Uncertainty: The regulatory landscape for cryptocurrencies varies by country and is continually evolving. Changes in regulations can impact the legality and taxation of crypto holdings.

Security Risks: Storing cryptocurrencies securely is critical. Hacks, scams, and thefts of crypto assets are not uncommon. Investors must use robust security practices, such as hardware wallets and strong passwords.

Lack of Consumer Protections: Unlike traditional financial systems, cryptocurrencies offer limited recourse for investors in case of disputes or losses. There are often no chargebacks or fraud protections.

Market Manipulation: Cryptocurrency markets are relatively young and less regulated than traditional financial markets. This can make them susceptible to market manipulation, pump and dump schemes, and insider trading.

Market Sentiment: Crypto prices can be highly influenced by market sentiment, news, and social media. This makes the market susceptible to hype and irrational exuberance, leading to price bubbles.

Technological Risks: Cryptocurrencies and blockchain technology are still evolving. There is a risk of unforeseen technical issues, such as software bugs or vulnerabilities.

Lack of Understanding: Many investors enter the crypto market without a full understanding of how cryptocurrencies and blockchain technology work. This lack of knowledge can lead to poor investment decisions.

Illiquidity: Some cryptocurrencies may have low trading volumes, making it challenging to buy or sell large amounts without significantly impacting the market price.

Taxation: The tax treatment of cryptocurrencies varies by jurisdiction and can be complex. Failing to report crypto gains accurately can result in legal and financial consequences.

In summary, crypto investing offers the potential for high returns, diversification, financial inclusion, and innovation. However, it also comes with risks such as extreme price volatility, regulatory uncertainty, security concerns, and lack of consumer protections. Before investing in cryptocurrencies, individuals should conduct thorough research, assess their risk tolerance, and consider seeking advice from financial professionals. Diversifying one's investment portfolio and adopting sound security practices are essential steps to mitigate risks associated with crypto investing.

Chapter 1: Understanding Cryptocurrency

What Is Cryptocurrency?

Cryptocurrency is a digital or virtual form of currency that uses cryptography for security. Unlike traditional fiat currencies (such as the US Dollar or Euro), cryptocurrencies are decentralized and typically operate on a technology called blockchain. Here are some key characteristics and components of cryptocurrencies:

Digital and Decentralized: Cryptocurrencies exist only in digital form, and they are not controlled by any central authority, government, or financial institution. Instead, they rely on a decentralized network of computers, often referred to as nodes or miners, to validate and record transactions.

Cryptography: Cryptocurrencies use cryptographic techniques to secure transactions and control the creation of new units. This cryptography ensures the integrity and confidentiality of transactions and provides the basis for the creation of digital wallets and addresses.

Blockchain Technology: Most cryptocurrencies operate on a blockchain, which is a distributed ledger that records all transactions across a network of computers. The blockchain is maintained by a consensus mechanism (e.g., proof of work or proof of stake) to ensure the accuracy and immutability of transaction data.

Limited Supply: Many cryptocurrencies have a predetermined supply limit, meaning there is a maximum number of coins or tokens that can ever be created. For example, Bitcoin has a cap of 21 million coins, which gives it a deflationary aspect.

Pseudonymity: Cryptocurrency transactions are pseudonymous, meaning that while transactions are recorded on the public blockchain, the identities of the parties involved are not necessarily tied to real-world identities. Instead, they use cryptographic addresses.

Global and Borderless: Cryptocurrencies can be used and transacted across national borders, providing a global means of exchange and reducing the need for traditional financial intermediaries in cross border transactions.

Peer to Peer Transactions: Cryptocurrencies enable peer to peer transactions without the need for intermediaries like banks. This can result in faster and potentially cheaper transfers of value.

Transparency: Blockchain technology provides transparency and immutability of transaction history. Anyone can view the entire transaction history of a cryptocurrency from its inception.

Use Cases: Cryptocurrencies have various use cases, including digital cash (e.g., Bitcoin), smart contracts (e.g., Ethereum), decentralized finance (DeFi), nonfungible tokens (NFTs), and more.

Volatility: Cryptocurrency prices are known for their volatility, with significant price fluctuations occurring over short periods. This can present both opportunities and risks for investors and users.

Some of the most well-known cryptocurrencies include Bitcoin (BTC), Ethereum (ETH), Ripple (XRP), Litecoin (LTC), and Bitcoin Cash (BCH), among others. Each cryptocurrency may have unique features and purposes, catering to different use cases and communities.

Overall, cryptocurrencies represent a fundamental shift in the way money and value are perceived and transacted. They offer the potential for financial innovation, increased accessibility to financial services, and new ways to interact with digital assets and contracts. However, they also come with risks and challenges, including regulatory concerns, security issues, and market volatility.

The History of Cryptocurrency

The history of cryptocurrency is a relatively short yet fascinating journey that has evolved over several decades. Here's a brief overview of the key milestones and developments in the history of cryptocurrency:

Pre-Bitcoin Era (1980s Early 2000s):

The concept of digital currency was explored as early as the 1980s, with various attempts to create cryptographic digital cash systems.

E-gold, founded in 1996, allowed users to open accounts and trade a digital representation of gold. It gained popularity but eventually faced legal issues and was shut down.

Bitcoin Emerges (2008):

In October 2008, an individual or group using the pseudonym "Satoshi Nakamoto" published the Bitcoin whitepaper titled "Bitcoin: A Peer-to-Peer Electronic Cash System."

On January 3, 2009, Nakamoto mined the first Bitcoin block, known as the "genesis block," marking the birth of Bitcoin.

Bitcoin introduced the concept of a decentralized digital currency, based on a blockchain, and it became the first widely adopted cryptocurrency.

Early Development and Adoption (2009-2012):

Bitcoin gained attention among cryptography and tech enthusiasts, leading to the creation of the first Bitcoin exchanges and early mining operations.

Bitcoin's value remained minimal initially, with some notable early transactions, such as the famous 10,000 BTC purchase of two pizzas in 2010.

Altcoins and Forks (2011-2013):

Litecoin, an early cryptocurrency designed to be a "lite" version of Bitcoin, was introduced in 2011.

Bitcoin experienced its first major software fork in 2013, resulting in the creation of Bitcoin Cash (BCH) and later, other Bitcoin forks.

Mainstream Awareness (2013-2017):

Bitcoin's price began to experience significant growth, leading to increased media attention and public awareness.

New cryptocurrencies, known as "altcoins," emerged, including Ethereum (ETH), which introduced smart contracts.

The Initial Coin Offering (ICO) boom started in 2017, allowing projects to raise funds by issuing their own tokens.

Crypto Boom and Bust (2017-2018):

Bitcoin reached an all-time high price near $20,000 in December 2017, sparking a surge in interest and investment in cryptocurrencies.

However, this was followed by a sharp market correction in 2018, leading to a "crypto winter."

Continued Development (2018-Present):

Despite market volatility, cryptocurrency and blockchain technology continued to advance.

Institutional interest in cryptocurrencies grew, with investment firms and corporations exploring blockchain applications.

Governments and regulators worldwide began developing guidelines and regulations for cryptocurrencies.

The emergence of decentralized finance (DeFi) and nonfungible tokens (NFTs) expanded the use cases of blockchain technology.

The history of cryptocurrency is marked by innovation, controversy, and rapid evolution. Bitcoin remains the most well-known and widely adopted cryptocurrency, but thousands of other cryptocurrencies now exist, each with its unique features and purposes. Cryptocurrency and blockchain technology continue to shape the financial and technological landscapes, with ongoing developments in various industries and sectors.

Different Types of Cryptocurrencies (Bitcoin, Ethereum, Altcoins)

There are thousands of different cryptocurrencies in existence, each with its own unique features, use cases, and underlying technologies. These cryptocurrencies can be broadly categorized into several types based on their characteristics and functions. Here are some of the main types of cryptocurrencies:

Bitcoin and Bitcoin Like Cryptocurrencies:

Bitcoin (BTC) was the first cryptocurrency and remains the most well-known and widely adopted. It serves primarily as a digital store of value and a medium of exchange.

Bitcoin like cryptocurrencies, often referred to as "altcoins," share similarities with Bitcoin but may have variations in features, such as faster transaction times or different consensus mechanisms. Examples include Litecoin (LTC) and Bitcoin Cash (BCH).

Smart Contract Platforms:

These cryptocurrencies, like Ethereum (ETH), enable the execution of smart contracts, which are self-executing contracts with the terms of the agreement directly written into code. They allow for decentralized applications (DApps) to be built on their platforms.

Privacy Coins:

Privacy focused cryptocurrencies, such as Monero (XMR), Zcash (ZEC), and Dash (DASH), prioritize user anonymity and the confidentiality of transactions. They use advanced cryptographic techniques to obscure transaction details.

Stablecoins:

Stablecoins are designed to have a stable value, often pegged to a fiat currency like the US Dollar (USD) or a commodity like gold. Tether (USDT), USD Coin (USDC), and DAI are examples of stablecoins.

Utility Tokens:

Utility tokens are used within a specific blockchain ecosystem to access and utilize certain services or products. For example, the Binance Coin (BNB) is used on the Binance exchange to pay for trading fees and other services.

Security Tokens:

Security tokens represent ownership in real-world assets, such as real estate, company shares, or investment funds. They are regulated and subject to securities laws in many jurisdictions.

Non-Fungible Tokens (NFTs):

NFTs are unique digital assets that represent ownership or proof of authenticity of a specific item, often digital art, collectibles, or in game items. Ethereum's ERC721 and ERC1155 standards are commonly used for NFTs.

Governance Tokens:

Governance tokens provide holders with voting rights in decentralized autonomous organizations (DAOs) and blockchain governance decisions. Examples include Maker Dao's MKR and Compound's COMP tokens.

Platform Tokens:

These tokens are native to specific blockchain platforms and may serve various purposes, such as transaction fees, network security, and staking rewards. Examples include Cardano's ADA and Polka dots DOT.

Cross Chain and Interoperability Tokens:

These tokens aim to facilitate interoperability between different blockchain networks, enabling assets and data to move seamlessly between blockchains. Examples include Chain-link (LINK) and Cosmos (ATOM).

Central Bank Digital Currencies (CBDCs):

Some countries are exploring the creation of their own digital currencies, known as CBDCs, which are typically issued and regulated by central banks. These are not traditional cryptocurrencies but digital representations of national currencies.

These are just a few of the many types of cryptocurrencies in existence. The cryptocurrency landscape continues to evolve, with new projects and tokens emerging regularly, each attempting to address specific use cases and challenges within the blockchain and digital asset space. Investors and users should carefully research and understand the unique features and purposes of different cryptocurrencies before getting involved.

How Cryptocurrencies Work (Blockchain Technology)

Cryptocurrencies work on the principles of blockchain technology, which is a decentralized and distributed ledger system. Here's a simplified explanation of how cryptocurrencies work:

Decentralization: Unlike traditional currencies that are controlled by central banks or governments, cryptocurrencies are decentralized. They operate on a network of computers (nodes) distributed across the globe. These nodes work together to maintain and validate the cryptocurrency's transactions and records.

Blockchain Technology: Cryptocurrencies rely on blockchain technology. A blockchain is a public ledger that records all transactions made with a particular cryptocurrency. It consists of a chain of blocks, each containing a group of transactions. Once a block is added to the chain, it cannot be altered, ensuring the security and immutability of the transaction history.

Cryptographic Security: Cryptocurrencies use cryptographic techniques to secure transactions and control the creation of new units. Public and private keys are used to facilitate secure transactions. The public key, known as an address, is used to receive funds, while the private key is kept secret and used to sign and authorize transactions.

Transactions: When a user wants to send cryptocurrency to another user, they create a transaction. This transaction includes the recipient's public key (address), the amount to be transferred, and a digital signature created with their private key. This signature serves as proof of ownership and authorization.

Mining and Consensus: Transactions are grouped together into blocks, and miners compete to solve complex mathematical puzzles to add a new block to the blockchain. This process is called mining and requires significant computational power. Once a block is successfully mined, it is added to the blockchain, and the miner is rewarded with newly created cryptocurrency (known as the block reward) and transaction fees.

Verification: Nodes on the network verify transactions to ensure they are legitimate and follow the rules of the cryptocurrency's protocol. If a transaction is valid, it is added to the pending block for inclusion in the blockchain.

Immutability: Once a transaction is recorded on the blockchain, it becomes permanent and cannot be altered. This immutability and transparency make it extremely difficult for anyone to manipulate the transaction history.

Peer to Peer Transactions: Cryptocurrencies enable direct peer to peer transactions without the need for intermediaries like banks. Users can send cryptocurrency to anyone with a compatible wallet address anywhere in the world, usually with lower transaction fees and faster settlement times compared to traditional financial systems.

Wallets: To store, manage, and transact with cryptocurrencies, users need a digital wallet. Wallets can be software based (online or mobile apps) or hardware based (physical devices). Wallets store the user's private keys, allowing them to access and control their cryptocurrency holdings.

Public Ledger: The blockchain is publicly accessible, allowing anyone to view the transaction history and check the balances of addresses. However, users' identities are typically pseudonymous, represented by cryptographic addresses rather than personal information.

This is a simplified overview of how cryptocurrencies work. The specific mechanics can vary depending on the cryptocurrency's protocol and underlying technology. Cryptocurrencies have evolved to serve various purposes beyond digital cash, including smart contracts, decentralized applications, and more. Their decentralized, secure, and transparent nature has led to their adoption in a wide range of industries and use cases.

Chapter 2: Why Invest in Cryptocurrency?

Investing in cryptocurrency can be a compelling option for some individuals, but it's essential to consider the potential benefits and risks carefully. Here are several reasons why people choose to invest in cryptocurrencies:

High Potential Returns: Cryptocurrencies have shown the potential for significant price appreciation over relatively short periods. Early investors in cryptocurrencies like Bitcoin have seen substantial gains in the past.

Diversification: Cryptocurrencies offer a unique asset class that may not be correlated with traditional investments like stocks and bonds. Including cryptocurrencies in an investment portfolio can help diversify risk.

Hedge Against Inflation: Some investors see cryptocurrencies, particularly Bitcoin, as a hedge against inflation and currency devaluation. The limited supply of cryptocurrencies can make them resistant to the effects of inflation.

Decentralization and Autonomy: Cryptocurrencies operate on decentralized networks, reducing the influence of central authorities. This appeals to individuals who value financial autonomy and control over their assets.

Global Accessibility: Cryptocurrencies can be bought, sold, and transferred globally, providing access to financial services and assets for individuals in regions with limited banking infrastructure.

Financial Inclusion: Cryptocurrencies have the potential to bring financial services to the unbanked and underbanked populations, providing an inclusive and accessible financial system.

Innovation: Beyond serving as digital currencies, cryptocurrencies and blockchain technology underpin innovations such as smart contracts, decentralized finance (DeFi), nonfungible tokens (NFTs), and more.

Speculative Potential: Some investors are attracted to the speculative potential of cryptocurrencies, aiming to profit from price volatility and market dynamics.

Early Adoption: Believers in the long-term potential of blockchain technology and cryptocurrencies may choose to invest early in projects they find promising.

Financial Education: Investing in cryptocurrencies can be an educational experience, helping individuals learn about blockchain technology, economics, and financial markets.

While there are potential benefits to investing in cryptocurrencies, it's crucial to acknowledge the associated risks:

Volatility: Cryptocurrency prices are highly volatile, and significant price fluctuations can lead to substantial gains or losses.

Regulatory Uncertainty: The regulatory environment for cryptocurrencies varies by country and is continually evolving. Changes in regulations can impact the legality and taxation of cryptocurrencies.

Security Risks: Storing cryptocurrencies securely is critical, as they are susceptible to theft and hacking. Proper security measures, such as hardware wallets and strong passwords, are essential.

Lack of Consumer Protections: Unlike traditional financial systems, cryptocurrencies often offer limited recourse in case of disputes or losses.

Market Speculation: The cryptocurrency market can be influenced by market sentiment, news, and social media, leading to irrational exuberance and price bubbles.

Technological Risks: Cryptocurrencies and blockchain technology are still evolving, and there is a risk of technical issues, vulnerabilities, and software bugs.

Lack of Understanding: Many individuals invest in cryptocurrencies without a full understanding of how they work, which can lead to poor investment decisions.

Before investing in cryptocurrencies, individuals should conduct thorough research, understand their risk tolerance, and consider seeking advice from financial professionals. Diversifying one's investment portfolio and adopting sound security practices are also crucial steps to mitigate risks associated with cryptocurrency investments.

Chapter 3: Getting Started with Crypto

Getting started with cryptocurrency involves several key steps to ensure that you understand the basics, invest safely, and protect your assets. Here's a step-by-step guide to help you get started:

Educate Yourself:

Before investing in cryptocurrency, take the time to learn about the technology, different cryptocurrencies, and how blockchain works. There are numerous online resources, courses, and books available to help you get started.

Determine Your Investment Goals and Risk Tolerance:

Clarify your reasons for investing in cryptocurrencies. Are you looking for long-term growth, short-term gains, or diversification? Assess your risk tolerance to determine how much you can comfortably invest.

Choose a Reliable Exchange:

To buy, sell, and trade cryptocurrencies, you'll need to choose a reputable cryptocurrency exchange. Look for exchanges with a strong track record, security features, and a user-friendly interface. Some popular options include Coinbase, Binance, Kraken, and Gemini.

Complete the Verification Process:

Most exchanges require users to verify their identity before trading or withdrawing funds. This typically involves providing identification documents, proof of address, and sometimes a selfie with your ID.

Set Up a Secure Wallet:

To store your cryptocurrencies securely, you'll need a digital wallet. There are various types of wallets, including software wallets (online, mobile, desktop) and hardware wallets (physical devices). Hardware wallets are often considered the most secure option for long-term storage.

Start with a Small Investment:

If you're new to cryptocurrency investing, consider starting with a small amount of money that you can afford to lose. This allows you to gain experience without risking a significant portion of your capital.

Buy Cryptocurrency:

Use the exchange to purchase cryptocurrency of your choice. You can typically fund your exchange account with fiat currency (e.g., USD, EUR) or trade other cryptocurrencies for the one you want to invest in.

Secure Your Investments:

Implement strong security practices to protect your investments. This includes enabling two factor authentication (2FA) on your exchange and wallet accounts, using complex passwords, and regularly updating your security measures.

Stay Informed:

Keep up to date with the latest news and developments in the cryptocurrency space. Market sentiment and news can impact prices and trends.

Consider a Diversified Portfolio:

While Bitcoin is the most well-known cryptocurrency, consider diversifying your portfolio by investing in other cryptocurrencies that align with your investment goals.

Understand Tax Implications:

Cryptocurrency transactions may have tax implications, depending on your country's regulations. Be aware of tax reporting requirements and consult with a tax professional if needed.

Have an Exit Strategy:

Decide in advance when you plan to sell your cryptocurrency holdings, and under what conditions. Avoid making impulsive decisions based on market fluctuations.

Avoid FOMO and Panic Selling:

Emotions like fear of missing out (FOMO) and panic can lead to poor investment decisions. Stick to your investment strategy and avoid making rash moves in response to market volatility.

Remember that cryptocurrency investments carry risks, and the market can be highly volatile. It's essential to do your due diligence, be patient, and invest only what you can afford to lose. Cryptocurrency markets operate 24/7, so you can trade or manage your investments at any time, but be mindful of the potential for round-the-clock price fluctuations.

Chapter 4: Fundamental Analysis

Fundamental analysis of cryptocurrencies involves evaluating the underlying factors and data that affect the value and potential of a particular cryptocurrency. While cryptocurrencies don't have traditional financial statements like stocks, you can assess them using the following fundamental analysis principles:

Use Case and Utility:

Evaluate the cryptocurrency's use case and utility. What problem does it solve? Is it designed for peer-to-peer transactions, smart contracts, privacy, or other specific applications?

Assess whether the cryptocurrency has a real-world use and demand. A cryptocurrency with a practical and valuable use case is more likely to succeed.

Technology and Development Team:

Examine the technology behind the cryptocurrency and the qualifications of the development team. Are they actively improving the blockchain's functionality, security, and scalability?

Research the cryptocurrency's codebase and whether it undergoes regular updates and improvements.

Community and Adoption:

Monitor the size and engagement of the cryptocurrency's community. Active social media channels, forums, and developer communities can indicate strong support.

Analyze the adoption rate and partnerships. Are businesses, institutions, or other projects integrating or using the cryptocurrency?

Market Capitalization and Supply:

Determine the cryptocurrency's market capitalization, which is calculated by multiplying its current price by its total circulating supply. Higher market cap coins are often considered more stable.

Evaluate the supply dynamics, including token distribution, inflation rate, and whether the cryptocurrency follows a deflationary or inflationary model.

Competition and Market Position:

Research the competitive landscape. Are there similar cryptocurrencies addressing the same use case? Compare the cryptocurrency's technology, adoption, and community support to its competitors.

Assess the cryptocurrency's market position, including its rank among cryptocurrencies by market cap.

Security and Reliability:

Investigate the security measures in place to protect the cryptocurrency from vulnerabilities and hacks. Has it experienced significant security breaches or issues in the past?

Consider the reliability and stability of the blockchain network. Does it have a history of downtime or network congestion?

Regulatory and Legal Considerations:

Be aware of the regulatory environment in which the cryptocurrency operates. Changes in regulations can significantly impact the cryptocurrency's value and legality.

Determine whether the cryptocurrency complies with relevant legal and regulatory requirements in different jurisdictions.

Economic and Macroeconomic Factors:

Consider broader economic factors, such as interest rates, inflation, geopolitical events, and market sentiment, that may affect the cryptocurrency market as a whole.

News and Events:

Stay informed about news and events related to the cryptocurrency. Market moving news, partnerships, protocol upgrades, and security incidents can have a substantial impact on its value.

Valuation Models:

Some analysts use valuation models specific to cryptocurrencies, such as the Network Value to Transactions (NVT) ratio or the Stock to Flow model, to estimate the asset's fair value.

Token Governance and Decision Making:

Understand the governance model of the cryptocurrency, including how decisions are made and implemented. Some cryptocurrencies have decentralized autonomous organizations (DAOs) that enable token holders to participate in governance.

Remember that fundamental analysis, while informative, is just one aspect of evaluating a cryptocurrency's potential. Cryptocurrency markets are highly speculative and can be influenced by sentiment, market dynamics, and speculative trading. Therefore, it's advisable to combine fundamental analysis with other forms of analysis, such as technical analysis and sentiment analysis, to make well-informed investment decisions. Additionally, conducting thorough research and staying updated on market developments is essential for successful cryptocurrency investing.

Chapter 5: Technical Analysis

Technical analysis (TA) is a popular method for analyzing cryptocurrency price movements and making trading decisions based on historical price charts and market data. It involves studying patterns, trends, indicators, and other technical factors to predict future price movements. Here are the key components of technical analysis for cryptocurrencies:

Price Charts: Price charts are the foundation of technical analysis. Cryptocurrency traders use various types of charts, including line charts, bar charts, and candlestick charts, to visualize price data over time.

Timeframes: Traders can analyze cryptocurrency price charts at different timeframes, ranging from seconds (intraday trading) to days, weeks, or months (swing or long-term trading). Shorter timeframes are more suitable for day traders, while longer timeframes are used for long-term investing.

Candlestick Patterns: Candlestick charts are commonly used in cryptocurrency technical analysis. Traders look for specific candlestick patterns, such as doji, engulfing, and hammer patterns, to make predictions about price reversals or continuations.

Support and Resistance Levels: Support levels are price levels at which an asset tends to find buying interest, preventing it from falling further. Resistance levels are where selling pressure tends to emerge, preventing further price increases. Traders use these levels to identify potential entry and exit points.

Trend Analysis: Traders identify trends in cryptocurrency prices, which can be upward (bullish), downward (bearish), or sideways (rangebound). Trendlines are drawn to visualize trend directions and reversals.

Indicators: Technical indicators are mathematical calculations applied to price, volume, or open interest data. Common indicators for cryptocurrency analysis include Moving Averages (MAs), Relative Strength Index (RSI), Moving Average Convergence Divergence (MACD), and Bollinger Bands. These indicators help traders identify potential buy or sell signals.

Volume Analysis: Volume is an essential component of technical analysis. Traders analyze trading volume to confirm the validity of price movements. An increase in volume during a price move is often seen as a sign of a strong trend.

Chart Patterns: Chart patterns, such as triangles, head and shoulders, flags, and pennants, are formations that appear on price charts. Traders use these patterns to make predictions about future price movements.

Fibonacci Retracement: Fibonacci retracement levels are used to identify potential support and resistance levels based on Fibonacci ratios. Traders use these levels to determine where price corrections may occur.

Divergence: Divergence occurs when the price and an indicator move in opposite directions. Bullish divergence may indicate a potential price reversal to the upside, while bearish divergence suggests a potential downturn.

Ichimoku Cloud: The Ichimoku Cloud is a comprehensive indicator that provides information about support and resistance levels, trend direction, and potential buy or sell signals.

Crypto specific Metrics: Some cryptocurrencies have unique metrics and indicators specific to their networks. For example, on chain metrics, like transaction volume and active addresses, can provide insights into network activity.

It's important to note that technical analysis has its strengths and limitations. While it can help identify potential entry and exit points and provide insights into market sentiment, it's not foolproof, and past price data doesn't guarantee future performance. Traders should use technical analysis in conjunction with other forms of analysis, practice risk management, and continuously update their trading strategies to adapt to changing market conditions.

Chapter 6: Risk Management and Strategy

Trading cryptocurrencies can be highly rewarding, but it also involves significant risks due to the market's volatility and unpredictability. Effective risk management and a well-defined trading strategy are crucial to protect your capital and increase your chances of success. Here are some key principles for risk management and trading strategies when trading cryptocurrencies:

Risk Management:

Set a Risk Tolerance: Determine how much capital you are willing to risk on each trade or investment. Your risk tolerance should be based on your overall financial situation and investment goals.

Use Stoploss Orders: Implement stoploss orders to limit potential losses. A stoploss order automatically sells your cryptocurrency position if it reaches a certain price level, helping you avoid substantial losses.

Diversify Your Portfolio: Avoid putting all your capital into a single cryptocurrency. Diversify your investments across different assets to spread risk. This can include holding various cryptocurrencies or even traditional assets like stocks and bonds.

Position Sizing: Calculate the position size for each trade based on your risk tolerance and the distance to your stoploss level. This ensures that you don't overcommit to a single trade.

Risk Reward Ratio: Assess the potential risk and reward of each trade. A common rule of thumb is to aim for a risk reward ratio of at least 1:2. This means that the potential profit should be at least twice the potential loss.

Avoid Overleveraging: Leverage can amplify both gains and losses. Use leverage cautiously, if at all, and be aware of the liquidation price on leveraged positions.

Stay Informed: Keep up to date with news and events that could impact the cryptocurrency market. Sudden news developments can lead to rapid price swings, and being informed can help you make timely decisions.

Trading Strategies:

Develop a Trading Plan: Create a well-thought-out trading plan that includes entry and exit criteria, stoploss levels, position sizing rules, and a clear strategy for managing trades.

Choose a Trading Style: Decide on a trading style that suits your personality and schedule. Common styles include day trading, swing trading, and long-term investing. Each style requires a different approach and time commitment.

Technical Analysis: Use technical analysis tools and indicators to identify potential entry and exit points. Consider using multiple indicators to confirm signals and reduce false alarms.

Fundamental Analysis: Combine technical analysis with fundamental analysis to assess the long-term potential of the cryptocurrencies you're trading. Consider factors like use case, technology, adoption, and competition.

Risk Reward Management: Always assess the risk reward ratio before entering a trade. Only take trades that offer a favourable risk reward profile, and avoid chasing excessive gains.

Emotion Control: Emotions can lead to impulsive decisions. Stick to your trading plan and avoid making emotionally driven trades based on fear or greed.

Back testing: Test your trading strategies on historical data to assess their performance. This can help you refine your approach and identify strengths and weaknesses.

Continuous Learning: The cryptocurrency market is constantly evolving. Stay committed to learning and improving your trading skills. Consider joining trading communities, reading books, and attending webinars and conferences.

Paper Trading: If you're new to trading or trying out a new strategy, consider paper trading (simulated trading without real money) to practice without risking capital.

Adapt to Market Conditions: Be flexible and adapt your strategies to changing market conditions. What works in a bull market may not be effective in a bear market.

Remember that trading cryptocurrencies involves risks, and there are no guarantees of profit. It's essential to start with a small amount of capital, practice discipline, and continuously refine your approach as you gain experience. Additionally, consider consulting with financial professionals or mentors who can provide guidance and support in your trading journey.

Chapter 7: Trading Strategies

Cryptocurrency trading encompasses various strategies to suit different goals, risk tolerances, and timeframes. Here are some common trading strategies in the crypto market:

Long-term Investing:

   Objective: Long-term investors aim to buy cryptocurrencies with the intention of holding them for an extended period, typically years. They believe in the long-term potential of the assets.

   Approach: Long-term investors often conduct thorough fundamental analysis to select cryptocurrencies they believe will appreciate significantly over time. They are less concerned with short-term price fluctuations and may tolerate volatility.

Swing Trading:

   Objective: Swing traders seek to profit from short to medium-term price swings in cryptocurrencies. They aim to capitalize on both upward and downward price movements.

   Approach: Swing traders use technical and fundamental analysis to identify potential entry and exit points. They typically hold positions for several days to weeks, making fewer trades than day traders.

Day Trading:

Objective: Day traders buy and sell cryptocurrencies within the same trading day, aiming to profit from short-term price fluctuations. They rarely hold positions overnight.

Approach: Day traders rely heavily on technical analysis, chart patterns, and technical indicators to make quick decisions. They closely monitor price charts, execute multiple trades each day, and may use leverage.

HODLing:

Objective: HODLers are long-term investors who adopt a "hold" strategy, often motivated by the belief in the long-term success of a cryptocurrency. The term "HODL" originated from a misspelling of "hold."

Approach: HODLers buy cryptocurrencies and resist the urge to sell them, regardless of short-term price volatility. They are willing to endure market fluctuations with the expectation of significant future gains.

Each of these trading strategies comes with its advantages and challenges. It's important to choose a strategy that aligns with your risk tolerance, time commitment, and knowledge level. Here are some additional considerations:

Risk Management: Implement effective risk management techniques, such as setting stoploss orders and position sizing, regardless of your chosen strategy.

Continuous Learning: The cryptocurrency market is dynamic, and it's essential to stay informed about market developments, regulatory changes, and emerging technologies.

Emotion Control: Emotional discipline is crucial for successful trading. Avoid making impulsive decisions based on fear or greed.

Back testing and Strategy Refinement: Test your chosen strategy on historical data to evaluate its performance. Adjust and refine your strategy as needed based on your results.

Diversification: Consider diversifying your cryptocurrency holdings across different assets to spread risk, especially if you are a long-term investor.

Stay Informed: Keep up to date with news and events that could impact the cryptocurrency market. Be prepared to adapt your strategy in response to significant developments.

Remember that there are no guarantees in trading, and the cryptocurrency market can be highly volatile. It's advisable to start with a small amount of capital, practice discipline, and continuously improve your trading skills and strategies over time.

Chapter 8: Taxes and Regulations

Taxes and regulations related to cryptocurrencies can vary significantly depending on your country or jurisdiction. It's essential to understand and comply with the tax laws and regulations applicable to cryptocurrency transactions in your area. Here are some general principles and considerations:

Taxation of Cryptocurrency Transactions:

Income Tax: In many countries, cryptocurrency transactions, including buying, selling, and trading, can be subject to income tax. Profits made from cryptocurrency trading and investments are typically considered taxable income. You may be required to report these gains on your annual tax return.

Capital Gains Tax: Some countries treat cryptocurrency gains as capital gains, which are taxed at a different rate than regular income. The tax rate may depend on the duration of time you held the cryptocurrency before selling it (short-term vs. long-term capital gains).

Mining and Staking: If you mine or stake cryptocurrencies, the rewards you receive may be considered taxable income. You might be required to report the fair market value of the coins received at the time you received them.

Crypto to Crypto Transactions: Even transactions between different cryptocurrencies can be taxable events. These are typically subject to capital gains tax based on the fair market value at the time of the transaction.

Reporting and Compliance:

Keep Records: Maintain detailed records of all cryptocurrency transactions, including dates, amounts, counterparties, and transaction IDs. Proper recordkeeping is crucial for accurate tax reporting.

Annual Reporting: In most jurisdictions, you'll need to report your cryptocurrency holdings and transactions on your annual tax return. Failure to do so can result in penalties or legal consequences.

Third-party Reporting: Some cryptocurrency exchanges and service providers may report your transaction history to tax authorities, so it's essential to ensure that your reported income and gains align with these records.

Regulatory Compliance:

Anti-Money Laundering (AML) and Know Your Customer (KYC) Regulations: Many jurisdictions require cryptocurrency exchanges and service providers to implement AML and KYC procedures to prevent illegal activities, such as money laundering and terrorist financing.

Securities Regulations: Some cryptocurrencies and token offerings may be subject to securities regulations in your jurisdiction. Be aware of the legal status of the assets you're dealing with.

Tax Treatment of ICOs and Token Sales: The tax treatment of Initial Coin Offerings (ICOs) and token sales can vary. In some cases, the sale of tokens may be considered taxable income or subject to capital gains tax.

Consult a Tax Professional:

Given the complexity and evolving nature of cryptocurrency taxation and regulations, it's highly advisable to consult with a tax professional or accountant who specializes in cryptocurrency taxation in your jurisdiction. They can provide personalized guidance based on your specific circumstances and help you navigate the tax landscape.

Failure to comply with tax laws and regulations can lead to legal consequences, penalties, and fines. Therefore, it's essential to stay informed and ensure that you are meeting your tax obligations when dealing with cryptocurrencies. Additionally, regulations surrounding cryptocurrencies can change, so it's crucial to stay updated on any new developments or guidance issued by tax authorities.

Chapter 9: Security and Safety

Ensuring the security and safety of your cryptocurrencies is paramount due to the irreversible nature of blockchain transactions and the potential risks associated with digital assets. Here are essential security practices to protect your cryptocurrency holdings:

Use a Hardware Wallet:

Hardware wallets are physical devices designed to store your cryptocurrencies offline. They provide an extra layer of security by keeping your private keys offline, making them resistant to online hacking attempts.

Enable Two Factor Authentication (2FA):

Enable 2FA on all your cryptocurrency exchange and wallet accounts. This adds an extra layer of security by requiring a onetime code from a secondary device (e.g., a mobile app or hardware token) to access your accounts.

Choose Strong, Unique Passwords:

Create strong, complex passwords for your cryptocurrency accounts. Avoid using easily guessable passwords or repeating passwords across multiple accounts. Consider using a reputable password manager to generate and store your passwords securely.

Keep Software Updated:

Regularly update the software of your cryptocurrency wallet, exchange accounts, and any associated applications. Updates often include security patches that address vulnerabilities.

Be Cautious with Phishing Attempts:

Be vigilant about phishing attempts. Avoid clicking on suspicious links or providing sensitive information to unknown sources. Verify the authenticity of websites and communications.

Use Secure Networks:

When accessing your cryptocurrency accounts, use secure and private networks. Avoid using public WIFI networks, which may expose you to potential security risks.

Be Wary of Social Engineering:

Be cautious of social engineering attempts, such as impersonation or manipulation tactics used by attackers to gain access to your accounts or private keys.

Backup Your Wallet:

Regularly back up your wallet's private keys or seed phrases in multiple secure locations. Ensure that the backup is stored in a place that is both physically and digitally secure.

Implement a Multi-signature Wallet:

Consider using a multi-signature wallet, which requires multiple private keys to authorize transactions. This can enhance security by requiring the cooperation of multiple parties.

Use Cold Storage:

For long-term storage of significant cryptocurrency holdings, consider using cold storage solutions, such as paper wallets or hardware wallets. Cold storage keeps your private keys offline, making them immune to online attacks.

Educate Yourself:

Continuously educate yourself about security best practices in the cryptocurrency space. Stay informed about the latest security threats and developments.

Double Check Addresses:

Before sending cryptocurrency, doublecheck the recipient's wallet address to ensure accuracy. Sending funds to the wrong address can result in irreversible loss.

Consider Insurance:

Some cryptocurrency exchanges and custodial services offer insurance coverage for digital assets. Consider using services with insurance to protect your holdings.

Limit Exposure:

Avoid disclosing the size of your cryptocurrency holdings or other sensitive information publicly. Limit your exposure to potential threats by practicing discretion.

Prepare for Inheritance:

Make arrangements for the secure transfer of your cryptocurrency holdings in case of your incapacitation or passing. This may involve providing access instructions to trusted individuals or using a service that offers estate planning for digital assets.

Remember that cryptocurrency security is your responsibility, and there is no recourse for recovering lost or stolen funds in many cases. By following these security practices and staying vigilant, you can significantly reduce the risks associated with owning and transacting in cryptocurrencies.

Chapter 10: Overcoming Challenges

Overcoming challenges in the cryptocurrency market requires a combination of knowledge, discipline, and adaptability. Here are some strategies to address common challenges when dealing with cryptocurrencies:

Dealing with Market Volatility:

Diversify Your Portfolio: Spreading your investments across different cryptocurrencies can help mitigate the impact of volatility. A diversified portfolio is less likely to be affected by a single asset's price swings.

Set Realistic Expectations: Understand that cryptocurrency markets are highly volatile and can experience rapid price fluctuations. Avoid making impulsive decisions based on short-term price movements.

Implement Risk Management: Use stoploss orders, position sizing, and risk reward ratios to manage your exposure to potential losses. Setting predefined exit points can help protect your capital.

HODLing Strategy: Consider a long-term HODLing strategy if you believe in the fundamental value of a cryptocurrency. HODLing involves holding assets through market volatility with the expectation of long-term gains.

Emotional Resilience:

Stay Calm and Patient: Emotions like fear and greed can lead to impulsive decisions. Develop emotional discipline by sticking to your trading plan and avoiding rash moves in response to market fluctuations.

Practice Mindfulness: Take breaks, meditate, or practice mindfulness techniques to maintain emotional balance while trading. Avoid checking prices obsessively, as this can lead to stress and anxiety.

Avoid Overtrading: Overtrading can result from emotional reactions to market movements. Stick to a well-defined trading plan and avoid excessive trading that can lead to exhaustion and poor decision-making.

Staying Informed:

Continuous Learning: The cryptocurrency market is constantly evolving. Dedicate time to learning about blockchain technology, market trends, and new developments. Stay updated on news and events that can impact prices.

Join Communities: Engage with cryptocurrency communities, forums, and social media groups. Participating in discussions and sharing insights with others can help you stay informed and gain different perspectives.

Follow Influential Figures: Follow influential figures and thought leaders in the cryptocurrency space. They often provide valuable insights and analysis through blogs, podcasts, and social media.

Learning from Mistakes:

Keep a Trading Journal: Maintain a detailed trading journal to record your trades, decisions, and the outcomes. Review your journal regularly to identify patterns and learn from both successful and unsuccessful trades.

Seek Feedback: Share your trading experiences with experienced traders or mentors who can provide constructive feedback and guidance.

Adapt and Improve: Use your past mistakes as learning opportunities. Adapt your trading strategy, risk management, and decision-making process to avoid repeating the same errors.

Accept Responsibility: Take responsibility for your trading decisions and outcomes. Avoid blaming external factors or seeking scapegoats for losses.

Remember that overcoming challenges in cryptocurrency trading is an ongoing process. It's essential to approach the market with a mindset of continuous improvement, adaptability, and discipline. Additionally, consider seeking advice from experienced traders or financial professionals who can offer guidance and support as you navigate the cryptocurrency landscape.

Chapter 11: Case Studies

Real-life Success Stories

There are several real-life cryptocurrency success stories where individuals and companies have achieved significant financial gains or made significant contributions to the crypto space. Here are a few notable examples:

Bitcoin Early Adopters:

Some of the earliest adopters and miners of Bitcoin, like Satoshi Nakamoto (the pseudonymous creator of Bitcoin), who mined a significant number of early Bitcoin blocks, have potentially amassed substantial wealth due to Bitcoin's remarkable price appreciation.

Winklevoss Twins:

Cameron and Tyler Winklevoss, known for their legal battle with Mark Zuckerberg over the creation of Facebook, invested heavily in Bitcoin in its early days. They became prominent figures in the cryptocurrency space and founded the cryptocurrency exchange Gemini.

Barry Silbert:

Barry Silbert, the founder and CEO of Digital Currency Group (DCG), has been a major figure in the crypto industry. DCG has invested in numerous crypto related companies, including Coinbase, and Silbert is recognized for his role in promoting the adoption of digital assets.

Ethereum Cofounders:

Vitalik Buterin and other cofounders of Ethereum have played a pivotal role in the development of the Ethereum blockchain and its associated technologies. Ethereum has become one of the leading blockchain platforms and has given rise to a multitude of decentralized applications (dApps) and tokens.

Early Bitcoin Miners:

Some early Bitcoin miners who mined or acquired Bitcoin when it was relatively unknown and cheap have seen their holdings appreciate significantly. Several individuals and mining companies have amassed substantial wealth through their Bitcoin holdings.

Binance and Changpeng Zhao (CZ):

Binance, founded by Changpeng Zhao (CZ), has grown to become one of the largest cryptocurrency exchanges globally. CZ's leadership has played a pivotal role in the exchange's success, and Binance has expanded its services to include various crypto related products.

Ripple and XRP:

Ripple, the company behind the XRP cryptocurrency, has been successful in forging partnerships with financial institutions and banks. XRP has also gained attention as a digital asset for cross border payments.

Chain-link and Sergey Nazarov:

Chain-link, led by Sergey Nazarov, has become a leader in the decentralized oracle space. Its technology facilitates the integration of real-world data into smart contracts, enabling a wide range of applications across industries.

Cryptocurrency Traders and Investors:

Many individual cryptocurrency traders and investors have achieved substantial financial success by correctly timing their investments and trading strategies, taking advantage of market trends and opportunities.

Decentralized Finance (DeFi) Innovators:

DeFi pioneers and developers have created decentralized lending, borrowing, and trading platforms that have attracted billions of dollars in assets. Some of these innovators have profited from their involvement in DeFi projects.

These success stories highlight the potential for individuals and companies to achieve significant success in the cryptocurrency space through innovation, early adoption, and strategic investments. However, it's important to note that the crypto market is highly speculative and volatile, and not all participants experience such success. It often involves a high degree of risk and uncertainty.

Lessons Learned from Famous Crypto Investors

Famous crypto investors and traders have shared valuable lessons and insights from their experiences in the cryptocurrency market. Here are some lessons learned from a few notable crypto investors:

1. HODLing Through Volatility (HODL Strategy):

The term "HODL" originated from a misspelling of "hold" and represents a long-term holding strategy. Many successful investors emphasize the importance of patience and holding onto assets through market volatility. They believe in the long-term potential of cryptocurrencies.

2. Risk Management is Key:

Risk management is a fundamental principle stressed by many successful investors. It involves setting stoploss orders, diversifying portfolios, and not investing more than you can afford to lose. Protecting capital is often seen as more important than pursuing high returns.

3. Continuous Learning and Adaptation:

The cryptocurrency market is dynamic, and staying informed is crucial. Successful investors emphasize the need for continuous learning, adapting to market conditions, and staying updated on technological developments and market trends.

4. Emotional Discipline:

Emotions like fear and greed can lead to impulsive decisions. Many investors stress the importance of emotional discipline and the need to stick to a well-defined trading or investment plan, regardless of market sentiment.

5. Diversification Across Assets:

Diversifying investments across different cryptocurrencies can help spread risk. Successful investors often hold a mix of assets to mitigate the impact of individual asset price fluctuations.

6. Avoiding Overtrading:

Overtrading can lead to exhaustion and poor decision-making. Experienced investors recommend avoiding excessive trading and focusing on quality over quantity when making trades.

7. Staying Cautious of ICOs and Altcoins:

Initial Coin Offerings (ICOs) and lesser-known altcoins can be high-risk investments. Many seasoned investors advise caution when considering these assets and emphasize conducting thorough due diligence.

8. Security is Paramount:

Protecting your cryptocurrency holdings is critical. Using hardware wallets, enabling two factor authentication, and following strong security practices can help safeguard your assets from theft and hacking.

9. Understand the Technology:

Successful investors stress the importance of understanding the underlying technology of cryptocurrencies and blockchain. Knowledge about how these technologies work can inform investment decisions and reduce reliance on speculation.

10. Long Term Vision:

Many crypto investors adopt a long-term perspective, believing in the transformative potential of blockchain technology and cryptocurrencies over time. They don't get discouraged by short-term market fluctuations.

11. Community and Network Building:

Building relationships within the crypto community and networking with likeminded individuals can provide valuable insights, opportunities, and support.

12. Expect Regulatory Changes:

Regulatory changes in the crypto space are inevitable. Investors advise staying informed about evolving regulations and compliance requirements, as they can have a significant impact on the market.

13. Seek Professional Advice:

Some investors consult with financial professionals or tax experts who specialize in cryptocurrency investments to navigate complex regulatory and tax issues.

It's important to note that success in the cryptocurrency market is never guaranteed, and the market is highly speculative and volatile. What works for one investor may not work for another, and there are inherent risks involved. Therefore, it's crucial to conduct thorough research, understand your risk tolerance, and make informed decisions when participating in the cryptocurrency market.

Chapter 12: The Future of Crypto

The future of cryptocurrency is a dynamic and evolving landscape that encompasses various trends, emerging technologies, potential regulatory changes, and growing adoption in mainstream finance. Here are key considerations for each of these aspects:

Trends and Emerging Technologies:

Decentralized Finance (DeFi): DeFi has gained significant traction, allowing users to access financial services like lending, borrowing, and trading without traditional intermediaries. The growth of DeFi projects and platforms is likely to continue, offering innovative financial solutions.

Non-Fungible Tokens (NFTs): NFTs have gained widespread attention for their use in digital art, collectibles, and gaming. The NFT space is evolving, with potential applications beyond the art world, such as in real estate, music, and virtual reality.

Layer 2 Scaling Solutions: To address scalability issues and high transaction fees on certain blockchain networks (e.g., Ethereum), Layer 2 scaling solutions like rollups and sidechains are being developed to increase transaction throughput and reduce costs.

Cross Chain Compatibility: Cross chain protocols and technologies aim to facilitate interoperability between different blockchain networks, enabling assets and data to move seamlessly between platforms.

Central Bank Digital Currencies (CBDCs): Several countries are exploring the development of CBDCs, which are digital representations of national currencies. CBDCs could play a significant role in shaping the future of digital payments.

Smart Contracts Evolution: Smart contracts are becoming more versatile and programmable, allowing for more complex and automated financial agreements and applications.

Potential Regulatory Changes:

Global Regulatory Coordination: Regulatory frameworks for cryptocurrencies and blockchain technology are evolving worldwide. Expect greater coordination and harmonization of regulations as governments and international organizations seek to address issues like anti-money laundering (AML) and consumer protection.

Taxation: Tax authorities are increasingly focusing on cryptocurrency taxation. Expect clearer guidelines and reporting requirements for cryptocurrency transactions, including stricter enforcement.

Stablecoin Regulation: Stablecoins, which are often pegged to fiat currencies, face scrutiny from regulators concerned about their impact on monetary policy and financial stability. Regulations governing stablecoins are expected to emerge.

SEC and Crypto Securities: In the United States, the Securities and Exchange Commission (SEC) is actively regulating cryptocurrencies and tokens, particularly those deemed securities. This will likely shape the legal status of various digital assets.

Adoption in Mainstream Finance:

Institutional Investment: Institutional adoption of cryptocurrencies continues to grow, with more hedge funds, asset managers, and corporations adding Bitcoin and other digital assets to their portfolios.

Crypto Asset Integration: Traditional financial institutions are exploring ways to integrate cryptocurrencies and blockchain technology into their offerings, including custody services, trading platforms, and investment products.

Retail Use Cases: Cryptocurrencies are gaining acceptance as a means of payment for goods and services. Payment processors and merchants are increasingly allowing customers to transact in cryptocurrencies.

Digital Banking: Cryptocurrency focused banks and digital banking platforms are emerging, offering services such as crypto wallets, loans, and interest-bearing accounts.

Regulated Exchanges: Regulated cryptocurrency exchanges are becoming more common, providing a sense of security for traders and investors.

Education and Awareness: As awareness and understanding of cryptocurrencies grow, more individuals and businesses are likely to explore their potential uses and benefits.

It's important to note that the cryptocurrency landscape is still maturing, and uncertainties remain. The future of crypto will be shaped by ongoing developments in technology, regulations, and market dynamics. Individuals and organizations involved in the crypto space should stay informed, adapt to changes, and assess the potential impacts on their strategies and investments.

Chapter 13: Conclusion and Next Steps

Summing Up Key Points

Crypto investing has significant potential, including high returns, diversification benefits, decentralization, and financial inclusion. It can also drive innovation and has various use cases. However, it comes with notable risks, such as extreme price volatility, regulatory uncertainty, security issues, lack of consumer protections, market manipulation, and technological risks. Additionally, understanding the complex nature of cryptocurrencies and blockchain technology is crucial. Before investing, conduct thorough research, assess your risk tolerance, and consider seeking professional advice. Diversify your portfolio and prioritize robust security practices to mitigate these risks.

Encouragement for Ongoing Learning

Embracing the world of cryptocurrency is a journey filled with endless possibilities and opportunities for growth. Your commitment to learning about this dynamic and transformative field is commendable. Remember, every bit of knowledge you gain about cryptocurrency takes you one step closer to harnessing its potential. In an ever-evolving digital landscape, your dedication to staying informed and educated will not only empower you but also position you at the forefront of innovation. So, keep exploring, keep questioning, and keep pushing your boundaries. Your journey into the world of crypto is not just an investment in assets but an investment in your own future. With persistence and a hunger for knowledge, you're well on your way to mastering this exciting and revolutionary domain.

Resources and Further Reading

Online Courses and Tutorials:

Coursera: Offers courses on blockchain and cryptocurrencies from top universities.

edX: Provides a variety of blockchain and cryptocurrency related courses.

Khan Academy: Offers a beginner's course on Bitcoin and cryptocurrencies.

Crypto Zombies: An interactive coding school to learn blockchain development.

Books:

"Mastering Bitcoin" by Andreas M. Antonopoulos

"Mastering Ethereum" by Andreas M. Antonopoulos

"Blockchain Basics: A Non-Technical Introduction in 25 Steps" by Daniel Drescher

"The Internet of Money" by Andreas M. Antonopoulos (series of books)

YouTube Channels:

Andreas M. Antonopoulos: A renowned crypto educator.

Data Dash: Provides insights into cryptocurrency trading and investing.

aantonop: Andreas Antonopoulos' official YouTube channel.

Ivan on Tech: Covers various blockchain and crypto topics.

Cryptocurrency News and Analysis:

CoinDesk: Offers news, analysis, and events related to cryptocurrencies and blockchain technology.

Coin telegraph: Provides news, analysis, and educational content.

Crypto Slate: Offers news, research, and in-depth analysis.

Cryptocurrency Forums and Communities:

Bitcoin Talk: A popular forum for discussions on Bitcoin and other cryptocurrencies.

Reddit Cryptocurrency Subreddits: Subreddits like r/Bitcoin, r/Ethereum, and r/Cryptocurrency offer discussions and news.

Podcasts:

Unchained Podcast: Covers a wide range of blockchain and crypto topics.

The Pomp Podcast: Hosted by Anthony "Pomp" Pompliano, featuring crypto industry leaders.

Epicenter: Focuses on in-depth interviews with blockchain innovators.

Cryptocurrency Blogs:

Medium: Many blockchain and crypto experts publish articles here.

Coinbase Blog: Features educational content and updates on cryptocurrencies.

Blockchain.com Blog: Offers insights into blockchain technology.

Blockchain Development Resources:

Ethereum Developer Documentation: Essential for those interested in Ethereum development.

Bitcoin Developer Documentation: Resources for Bitcoin developers.

Truffle Suite: A development framework for Ethereum.

Social Media:

Follow reputable figures in the crypto space on Twitter for real-time updates and insights.

Local Meetups and Conferences:

Attend local blockchain and crypto meetups and conferences to network and learn from experts.

Online Forums:

Platforms like Stack Exchange have dedicated sections for blockchain and cryptocurrency related questions.

Whitepapers:

Read the original whitepapers of cryptocurrencies like Bitcoin and Ethereum for a deep understanding of their technology.

Remember that the cryptocurrency space is continually evolving, so staying informed through a variety of sources is crucial. Exercise caution and scepticism when exploring this field, and don't hesitate to seek advice from experts or professionals if you have specific questions or concerns. Happy learning!

Appendices:
Glossary of Crypto Terms

Blockchain: A decentralized and distributed ledger technology that records all transactions across a network of computers. It forms the foundation of cryptocurrencies.

Cryptocurrency: A digital or virtual currency that uses cryptography for security. Bitcoin, Ethereum, and Litecoin are examples.

Bitcoin (BTC): The first and most well-known cryptocurrency, created by an anonymous person or group known as Satoshi Nakamoto in 2009.

Altcoin: Any cryptocurrency other than Bitcoin. Examples include Ethereum (ETH), Ripple (XRP), and Litecoin (LTC).

Wallet: A digital tool or application used to store, send, and receive cryptocurrencies. Wallets can be software based (online or mobile) or hardware based (physical devices).

Public Key: A cryptographic key used to receive cryptocurrency into a wallet. It's a long alphanumeric string.

Private Key: A secret cryptographic key used to access and manage cryptocurrency in a wallet. It must be kept secure.

Decentralization: The principle of distributing control and authority across a network of computers, reducing the power of a central authority.

Mining: The process by which new cryptocurrencies are created and transactions are verified on a blockchain. Miners use computational power to solve complex mathematical puzzles.

Fork: A significant change in the protocol or rules of a blockchain. Forks can be hard (resulting in two separate blockchains) or soft (backwards compatible).

ICO (Initial Coin Offering): A fundraising method where new cryptocurrencies are sold to investors before being listed on exchanges.

Token: A digital asset built on an existing blockchain. Tokens can represent various things, including assets, utility, or ownership rights.

Smart Contract: Self executing contracts with the terms of the agreement between buyer and seller written directly into code on a blockchain.

HODL: A misspelling of "hold" often used in the crypto community to mean holding onto cryptocurrencies rather than selling them.

FOMO (Fear of Missing Out): The fear that you'll miss out on potential profits, leading to impulsive buying decisions.

FUD (Fear, Uncertainty, Doubt): Spreading negative or false information about a cryptocurrency to create fear and drive prices down.

ATH (All Time High): The highest price ever reached by a cryptocurrency.

Market Cap: The total value of a cryptocurrency calculated by multiplying its current price by the total supply of coins in circulation.

Whale: An individual or entity that holds a significant amount of cryptocurrency, capable of influencing market prices.

Satoshi: The smallest unit of Bitcoin, named after its creator, Satoshi Nakamoto. One Bitcoin is equal to 100 million Satoshi's.

Private Blockchain: A blockchain where access is restricted and controlled, often used by businesses and organizations.

Public Blockchain: A blockchain open to anyone, typically used for cryptocurrencies like Bitcoin and Ethereum.

Cold Wallet: A hardware wallet or offline storage device used to store cryptocurrency securely, disconnected from the internet.

Hot Wallet: An online or software-based wallet connected to the internet, suitable for day-to-day transactions.

DYOR (Do Your Own Research): Encouragement to thoroughly research and understand a cryptocurrency before investing.

These are just some of the many terms in the cryptocurrency space. As the field continues to evolve, new terms and concepts may emerge.

Additional Tools and Apps for Crypto Investors:

Here are some additional tools and apps that can be helpful for crypto investors:

Blockfolio: A popular cryptocurrency portfolio tracking app that allows you to monitor your holdings, view real time price data, and receive customizable alerts.

Delta: Similar to Blockfolio, Delta is a cryptocurrency portfolio tracker that offers portfolio management, price alerts, and detailed analytics.

CoinMarketCap: This website and mobile app provide comprehensive cryptocurrency market data, including price charts, market capitalization, trading volume, and historical data.

CoinGecko: An alternative to CoinMarketCap, CoinGecko offers cryptocurrency market data, along with additional features like DeFi tracking and NFT market information.

Crypto Exchanges Apps: Many cryptocurrency exchanges, such as Coinbase, Binance, Kraken, and Gemini, offer mobile apps for trading and managing your crypto assets on the go.

Crypto News Apps: Stay updated with the latest news and developments in the crypto space using apps like CryptoSlate, CoinDesk, or the News section of CoinMarketCap.

Trading View: A powerful charting platform that allows you to analyze cryptocurrency price movements with a wide range of technical indicators and drawing tools.

Coin Stats: A cryptocurrency portfolio and market tracking app that offers features like a news aggregator, watchlists, and a tax calculator.

Exodus: A multicurrency wallet with a built-in exchange feature that allows you to manage and trade various cryptocurrencies within the app.

Trust Wallet: A mobile wallet designed for Ethereum and ERC20 tokens, Trust Wallet offers a simple and secure way to store and manage your assets.

MyEtherWallet (MEW): A popular Ethereum wallet app that provides a user-friendly interface for managing Ethereum and Ethereum based tokens.

Hardware Wallet Apps: If you own a hardware wallet like Ledger Nano S or Trezor, their respective mobile apps can enhance security and provide access to your assets on the go.

Coin Tracking: A comprehensive cryptocurrency tax reporting and portfolio management tool that can help simplify tax season.

Cryptocurrency Payment Apps: Apps like Bit Pay and Coinomi enable you to make payments with cryptocurrencies at supported merchants.

NFT Wallets: If you're into nonfungible tokens (NFTs), consider wallets like MetaMask and Trust Wallet that support NFTs.

Crypto Tax Apps: Tools like CryptoTrader.Tax and CoinTracker help you calculate and report your cryptocurrency gains and losses for tax purposes.

Crypto Loan Apps: Platforms like Celsius and BlockFi offer mobile apps for earning interest on your crypto holdings or taking out crypto backed loans.

Cryptocurrency News Aggregators: Apps like Crypto News provide a curated feed of cryptocurrency news from various sources.

DeFi Apps: If you're interested in decentralized finance (DeFi), apps like Aave, Compound, and Uniswap offer DeFi services and can be accessed through their mobile apps.

Please exercise caution when using third party apps and ensure they are from reputable sources. Additionally, consider enabling two factor authentication (2FA) and practicing strong security measures to protect your cryptocurrency holdings.

Frequently Asked Questions

Here are some frequently asked questions (FAQs) about cryptocurrencies:

1. What is cryptocurrency?

Cryptocurrency is a digital or virtual form of currency that uses cryptography for security. It operates on a decentralized ledger called blockchain.

2. How does cryptocurrency work?

Cryptocurrencies work through a technology called blockchain, which is a distributed ledger that records all transactions across a network of computers. When a transaction is made, it is added to a block, which is then added to the blockchain after validation.

3. What is Bitcoin?

Bitcoin (BTC) is the first and most well-known cryptocurrency, created by an anonymous person or group known as Satoshi Nakamoto in 2009. It serves as a decentralized digital currency.

4. How do I buy cryptocurrency?

You can buy cryptocurrency on cryptocurrency exchanges using traditional fiat currency (like USD, EUR) or by exchanging another cryptocurrency.

Popular exchanges include Coinbase, Binance, and Kraken.

5. Where do I store my cryptocurrencies?

Cryptocurrencies are stored in digital wallets. These wallets can be hardware based (offline) or software based (online or mobile). Hardware wallets are considered more secure.

6. Are cryptocurrencies legal?

The legality of cryptocurrencies varies by country. Some countries have embraced them, while others have imposed restrictions or outright bans. It's essential to research and understand the regulations in your jurisdiction.

7. What is blockchain technology?

Blockchain is the underlying technology of cryptocurrencies. It is a decentralized and transparent ledger that records all transactions across a network of computers. It has various applications beyond cryptocurrencies, including supply chain management and smart contracts.

8. What are altcoins?

Altcoins are any cryptocurrencies other than Bitcoin. Examples include Ethereum (ETH), Ripple (XRP), Litecoin (LTC), and thousands of others.

9. What is a wallet address?

A wallet address is a unique string of characters used to receive cryptocurrency. It's essential to doublecheck addresses when making transactions to avoid sending funds to the wrong place.

10. Can I make money with cryptocurrency?

Yes, many people have made money through cryptocurrency investments, trading, and mining. However, it's a highly volatile and speculative market, so there are risks involved.

11. What are ICOs and STOs?

ICOs (Initial Coin Offerings) and STOs (Security Token Offerings) are fundraising methods in which new cryptocurrency tokens or digital securities are sold to investors. ICOs are less regulated, while STOs are subject to securities laws.

12. How do I stay safe in the cryptocurrency space?

Practice strong security measures, use reputable exchanges and wallets, enable two factor authentication (2FA), be cautious of phishing scams, and avoid sharing private keys or personal information.

13. What is the future of cryptocurrencies?

The future of cryptocurrencies is uncertain but promising. They have the potential to revolutionize finance, supply chains, and other industries. Regulatory developments and technological advancements will play a significant role in shaping their future.

14. How do I calculate taxes on cryptocurrency gains?

Cryptocurrency tax laws vary by country. It's essential to keep accurate records of your transactions and consult with a tax professional to ensure compliance with your local tax regulations.

15. Can I use cryptocurrencies for everyday purchases?

Some businesses and online retailers accept cryptocurrencies as a form of payment. However, it's not as widely accepted as traditional fiat currencies.

These FAQs cover some of the fundamental questions about cryptocurrencies, but the space is continually evolving, so it's essential to stay informed and conduct thorough research before getting involved.

www.ingramcontent.com/pod-product-compliance
Lightning Source LLC
Chambersburg PA
CBHW062352290526
45794CB00005B/2191